The Orphan of Zhao

James Fenton was born in Lincoln in 1949 and educated at Magdalen College, Oxford, where he won the Newdigate Prize for poetry. He has worked as political journalist, drama critic, book reviewer, war correspondent, foreign correspondent and columnist. He is a Fellow of the Royal Society of Literature and was Oxford Professor of Poetry for the period 1994–99. His poetry collections include *Children in Exile* and *Out of Danger*, for which he was awarded the Whitbread Prize. He wrote libretti for *Haroun and the Sea of Stories* (New York City Opera) and *Tsunami Song Cycle* (BBC Symphony Orchestra) and his theatre includes *Pictures from an Exhibition* (Young Vic) and *Tamar's Revenge* (Royal Shakespeare Company). In 2007 James Fenton was awarded the Queen's Gold Medal for Poetry. He is editor of *The New Faber Book of Love Poems*. *Yellow Tulips: Poems 1968–2011* was published by Faber and Faber in 2012.

by James Fenton from Faber

YELLOW TULIPS: POEMS 1968–2011

THE LOVE BOMB AND OTHER MUSICAL PIECES

THE NEW FABER BOOK OF LOVE POEMS

WILLIAM BLAKE: POET TO POET

SAMUEL TAYLOR COLERIDGE

CAMBODIAN WITNESS
The Autobiography of Someth May
(*editor*)

JAMES FENTON

The Orphan of Zhao

based on traditional Chinese sources

faber and faber

First published in 2012
by Faber and Faber Limited
74–77 Great Russell Street
London WC1B 3DA

Typeset by Country Setting, Kingsdown, Kent CT14 8ES
Printed and bound by CPI Group (UK) Ltd, Croydon CR0 4YY

A CIP record for this book
is available from the British Library

ISBN 978-0-571-30035-8

FSC
www.fsc.org
MIX
Paper from
responsible sources
FSC® C013604

2 4 6 8 10 9 7 5 3

Acknowledgements

There are innumerable versions of the story of *The Orphan of Zhao*: opera both in the Peking and in the Western tradition, film, radio drama, novel and theatre. Greg Doran, who asked me to write a new acting version, had already assembled a sample of them, including most notably Professors Stephen West and Wilt Idema's as yet unpublished translation of the 1615 text, which they very generously placed at our disposal.

At times I have followed this play closely, but in several major ways I have departed from it. To my Western ear, the word 'Duke' rings oddly in a Chinese feudal context, in a way that 'Emperor', 'Lord' and 'Princess' do not. I am not the first adapter to transfer the action from the court of a Duke to that of an Emperor, nor am I the first to allow the Princess to survive. I have set out to retell the story in the most telling way possible, avoiding none of the difficulties inherent in the material, but dwelling on the many dilemmas involved, and inventing freely.

I should like to thank Brian Holton, who translated the opera; Chenxin Jiang, who translated the Bayiji version; Beibei Zhan, who gave us a synopsis of the Story of the Eight Righteous People; and the family of Ma Lianliang, who sent us the Peking opera script. Dr Ruru Li gave us her guidance on Chinese theatrical practice. Professor Ralph Williams gave us lavish support during our workshop at Ann Arbor, Michigan, where the Confucius Institute mounted an intensive day-long event, examining the play.

I wrote this play, with its accompanying songs, while under the roof of the Cullman Center at New York Public Library, to whose director, Jean Strouse, and to whose staff I am most deeply indebted.

James Fenton

The RSC Ensemble is generously supported by
THE GATSBY CHARITABLE FOUNDATION
and THE KOVNER FOUNDATION

The RSC Literary Department is generously supported by
THE DRUE HEINZ TRUST

The Orphan of Zhao was first presented by the Royal Shakespeare Company at the Swan Theatre, Stratford-upon-Avon, on 30 October 2012. The cast, in alphabetical order, was as follows:

Ti Miming Matthew Aubrey
Ballad-Singer Jeremy Avis
The Princess Lucy Briggs-Owen
The Assassin, Chu Ni Adam Burton
Tu'an Gu Joe Dixon
Cheng Bo Jake Fairbrother
Dr Cheng Ying's Wife Nia Gwynne
Princess' Maid Susan Momoko Hingley
General Han Jue Lloyd Hutchinson
Gongsun Chujiu's Servant Joan Iyiola
Captain of the Guard Youssef Kerkour
Ghost of Dr Cheng Ying's Son Chris Lew Kum Hoi
Guard Siu Hun Li
Gongsun Chujiu Patrick Romer
Zhao Dun James Tucker
Dr Cheng Ying Graham Turner
The Emperor Stephen Ventura
Wei Jiang Philip Whitchurch

Musicians
   Ian Reynolds (flutes), Nicholas Lee (guitar),
   Ben Stevens (cello), Andrew Herbert, James Jones
   (percussion), Michael Keelan (keyboard/violin)

Directed by Gregory Doran
Designed by Niki Turner
Lighting designed by Tim Mitchell
Music by Paul Englishby
Sound designed by Martin Slavin
Movement Will Tuckett

Characters

The Emperor

Tu'an Gu
a powerful courtier, head of the Palace Guard

Zhao Dun
a minister and head of the Zhao clan,
married to the Emperor's daughter

Wei Jiang
a general and counsellor

Gongsun Chujiu
a counsellor

Han Jue
a general

Young Zhao *known as* **Cheng Bo**
the Orphan of Zhao, son of Zhao Dun,
sole survivor of his clan

The Princess
daughter of the Emperor,
wife of Zhao Dun, mother of the Orphan

Her Maid

Cheng Ying
a country doctor

Dr Cheng Ying's Wife

Chu Ni
an assassin sent to kill Zhao Dun

Ti Miming
a servant of Zhao Dun

Ballad-Singer

Captain of the Guard

Ghost of Dr Cheng Ying's Son

Guards, Soldiers, Eunuchs, Neighbours etc.

THE ORPHAN OF ZHAO

based on traditional Chinese sources

Part One

Ballad-Singer

> *Aiee, father of mine, father of mine,*
> *What are these shouts in the rain, these voices*
> *   in the air?*
> *The petal is ripped from the flower, the branch*
> *   from the tree.*
> *The torn limbs lie everywhere.*

The warriors come to the inn. They do not dismount.
They come from the north and they shout and they call
   for strong wine.
They point to the east and they point to the west and
   the south.
They point to the barn where you hide me, O father
   of mine.

> *Aiee, father of mine, father of mine,*
> *What are these shouts in the rain, these voices*
> *   in the air?*
> *The petal is ripped from the flower, the branch*
> *   from the tree.*
> *The torn limbs lie everywhere.*

You kiss me. You whisper. You bid me lie still in
   the grain.
You fill up the bowl from the jar. You go back to
   the yard.
And the warriors drink and they laugh in the heat
   of the wine.
There is blood on the saddle-cloth, blood on the
   sheath of the sword.

3

> *Aiee, father of mine, father of mine,*
> *What are these shouts in the rain, these voices*
>   *in the air?*
> *The petal is ripped from the flower, the branch*
>   *from the tree.*
> *The torn limbs lie everywhere.*

A magpie comes pushing its head through the thatch
  of the barn
And it hops to the bin and it pecks at the grain where
  I lie
And it pecks at the grain and it pecks at the face of
  your son
And they throw down the bowl and they run to the
  barn where I cry

Crying

> *Aiee, father of mine, father of mine,*
> *What are these shouts in the rain, these voices*
>   *in the air?*
> *The petal is ripped from the flower, the branch*
>   *from the tree.*
> *The torn limbs lie everywhere.*

*

He will mend the bowl with a wire. He cannot mend
  the heart.
He will pour out the wine from the jar. He will come
  to the grave
And from every tear that he pours, every drop that
  he spills,
I shall drink from the heat of the wine of his grief
  and his love.

SCENE TWO
THE DEMON MASTIFF

Tu'an Gu I am Tu'an Gu, head of the Palace Guard and one of the most powerful ministers at the Court of the Emperor of China.

'One of' – funny how much frustration can be conveyed by two simple words. One of the most, but not, somehow, *the* most powerful – it's a distinction hardly worth achieving. One of the most feared – but what's the use of being feared when there are others around who are more feared than you are? Or equally feared – so that a man may take care not to cross you, but, equally, may take care not to cross your chief rival and enemy.

'Equally' – there's another idiot word, as if there were any purpose in being another man's equal.

To be powerful, one must be feared, really feared. Not feared like some yapping little lapdog that we step gingerly past in the street, but feared like *this* dog . . .

He opens door on Demon Mastiff, which gives a terrifying display of hunger and rage.

Feared like the Demon Mastiff I have been training here in my compound. Nasty piece of work, isn't he? The sort of dog that makes you clutch at your throat for fear. A gift, this dog was, to the Emperor, from the Tibetan people, who said that this kind of mastiff has the power to sniff out treachery and deceit. Treachery and deceit! I said I'll take care of that. If there's treachery to be sniffed out, I'll be the one holding the leash.

Come here, boy. There! You have to know how to handle them, or you can lose a limb. Down! I said. Down, boy! Get them young enough, you can train any sort of dog.

That's what they say. And I got my hands on this dog in the nick of time. I keep it hungry, and here's how I train it. Once a week, a servant of mine makes a trip to the slaughterhouse and brings back, slung across his strong shoulders, two great buckets of offal. Tripe. Liver. Lungs. Blood, lots of it. All good stuff. The dog goes wild as the servant passes his cage.

The dog goes wild, of course he does. This is a hungry, angry dog. But here's where the training comes in. I set up three models made to look like ministers of the Court. The offal is hidden in one of them, and the dog's task is to sniff it out and go at it.

Well, this is a clever dog as well as a nasty piece of work. What the Demon Mastiff learnt very quickly was that the offal is always hidden in the figure with the purple robe. Watch.

Demon Mastiff, released from chain, goes straight for purple dummy, which it destroys in order to get at the offal.

That's what I call a well-trained dog. And if I were a minister in a purple robe, and I saw how this dog had been trained, I should be mortally afraid. I should clutch my throat for fear. That is, if I had time to clutch my throat, if I could see the fate that was being planned for me.

Heel, boy, heel. Back to your cage. Your moment is yet to come.

SCENE THREE
THE PEACH GARDEN MASSACRE

Enter Gongsun Chujiu, Wei Jiang and Zhao Dun.

Gongsun Chujiu This is the time of year when we travel out to the countryside to encourage the peasants to plough the fields and plant the crops. Come, Wei Jiang, Zhao Dun, let us go and perform the traditional rituals. In the old days of course the Emperor himself would always take part, and plough a symbolic furrow.

Wei Jiang Have you invited him, Gongsun?

Gongsun Chujiu I take care to do precisely that every year, but the invitation has to get past Tu'an Gu. The Emperor has never been keen on these ceremonies, though for us they are highly important. Without agriculture we would have no state.

Zhao Dun The Emperor is devoted to his pleasures, and Tu'an Gu understands him very well. He was the one who laid out the Peach Garden, sparing no expense, and his masterpiece has been the Crimson Cloud Tower – that tall building devoted to the pursuit of every pleasure, a place for banqueting, music and every form of sexual depravity.

Wei Jiang We seem to have become the Old Guard at the Court, always walking away from the festivities.

Gongsun Chujiu But someone at the Court must respect the ancient rituals. They bind us all together. Let us go and visit the farmers.

Exeunt. Tu'an Gu and the Emperor look down from the Crimson Cloud Tower.

Tu'an Gu As soon as the crowd heard that the Crimson Cloud Tower was to be opened today, they came flocking from all over the city.

Emperor How small they all look, like ants. I've never looked down on so many men before. They would make a fascinating target. Pass me my bow.

Tu'an Gu Your Majesty . . .

The Emperor begins shooting down into the crowd.

Emperor Like fish in a bowl. Here, Tu'an Gu. You aim at the crowd on the left. I'll shoot to the right. See? They don't know what's hitting them. You see that idiot looking around?

Tu'an Gu Now they're beginning to panic. They simply have no idea. What a sport.

Emperor There's one man looking up. He's seen us. I'll fix him, though.

Tu'an Gu Amazing shot. He's holding his face.

Emperor Now they're all looking up. They can't get away. The place is jammed. Give me more arrows.

Zhao Dun Where is the guard? There's a massacre down there. Some madman is shooting into the crowd.

Tu'an Gu Here, Zhao Dun. Have a go. The Emperor has invented a new sport.

Zhao Dun You murdering fool, have you gone crazy?

Tu'an Gu Are you addressing the Emperor?

Emperor We were just having a little fun.

Gongsun Chujiu What's going on here? Who has been shooting at the crowd?

Zhao Dun Be careful what you say.

Tu'an Gu You haven't answered my question, Zhao Dun. I asked you, when you used the words 'murdering fool', were you referring to the Emperor, your father-in-law . . . or to me?

Wei Jiang You don't need to answer him. He wants to trap you.

Gongsun Chujiu But an emperor who shoots his own subjects for sport? What is such a ruler to be called?

Emperor Oh, spare me the sight of this tedious old counsellor. I have had quite enough of his wisdom.

Tu'an Gu You hear that, Gongsun?

Gongsun Chujiu Yes, indeed I have heard that, and I shall, with the Emperor's permission, leave the Court forthwith, and retire.

Emperor An excellent idea. Go and practise virtue on your farm. I'm sick of sermons.

Wei Jiang Your Majesty, if Gongsun Chujiu is to be exiled from the Court, I too would prefer to go back to where I am most at home. I am a soldier, and there is plenty of work for me to do, guarding the borders of Your Majesty's empire. The city is like a prison to me. Let me go back to the mountains.

Emperor Wei Jiang, Wei Jiang, my dear general, not you as well? You had promised to teach me more of the arts of war.

Wei Jiang It seems there is little more I can teach you.

Emperor No, I can see from your expression there won't be much more fun with you. But you liked me once. You used to play with me.

Wei Jiang You have a new playmate now.

Tu'an Gu And now, Zhao Dun, your friends have left the Court. Maybe you too will want to pursue the rural life?

Zhao Dun My place is here at Court. I have no plans for retirement.

Exit.

Tu'an Gu But *I* have plans, Zhao Dun. I have plans.

SCENE FOUR
A RELUCTANT ASSASSIN

Tu'an Gu Chu Ni, a word with you.

Chu Ni Your Excellency.

Tu'an Gu I have always been good to you, haven't I?

Chu Ni I am deeply grateful to you. My obligation is enormous.

Tu'an Gu There is something I need you to do for me. It is important. Dare you undertake it?

Chu Ni For you, sir, I would go through fire and water.

Tu'an Gu Zhao Dun has insulted the Emperor. The Emperor commands you to assassinate him.

Chu Ni My lord.

Tu'an Gu You seem reluctant to obey the Emperor.

Chu Ni I will do it.

Tu'an Gu Go to his house tonight. Take him by surprise. Kill him. You will be very well rewarded.

Chu Ni I will obey.

Tu'an Gu Stop. Come back. If you fail in this, do not expect to live long.

Chu Ni I understand.

They part.

The Emperor commands! The Emperor commands me! I do not think the Emperor knows much about this. I do not think he plans to assassinate his son-in-law. I do not think Zhao Dun has insulted the Emperor or deceived the nation. But what can I do? I am bound to obey Tu'an Gu. Here is Zhao Dun's house. I will conceal myself behind this pagoda tree.

Enter Zhao Dun and the Princess.

Zhao Dun It is cool in the garden, and you, my dear wife, are with child. Go in now and leave me alone here to pray a while.

Princess You are worried. I know that. Something happened today in the Peach Garden, and people were killed. Were you in danger?

Zhao Dun I was not in danger, but we will all be in danger if your father continues to listen to Tu'an Gu. Go in now.

Princess I will obey you, but I do not like to leave you alone with these heavy thoughts.

Zhao Dun Ti Miming! Bring me the incense-burner, if you please. Set it over there. Now you may leave me.

Chu Ni This is my chance. He is alone.

Zhao Dun The moon is weak tonight, and the starlight dim, as I kneel in the dust before the incense-burner to pray for my country. Day and night, it worries me. I wish the Emperor would change his ways, stop listening to his favourites and toadies, start listening to loyal advice.

Chu Ni My hand is on my dagger. Yet something prevents me.

Zhao Dun Let the empire be governed by a wise ruler and honest advisers, our soldiers and our officials be faithful and true, hold back the raging seas to keep our country safe, wash all injustice clean for every subject.

The night is dark now and I must return to my rooms.

Chu Ni Sir!

Zhao Dun Who are you, blocking my path? I cannot see your face.

Chu Ni My name is Chu Ni, a servant in the house of Tu'an Gu. Today he ordered me to kill you.

Zhao Dun I am here, alone and unarmed. What has prevented you from doing so?

Chu Ni I heard you praying, and knew you to be an honest man. I cannot raise my hand against you.

Zhao Dun And if you disobey your orders?

Chu Ni Go in now, sir, and go to bed. I shall resolve this problem.

Zhao Dun Good night, my friend.

Chu Ni dashes his head against a tree. Servants come out of the house.

Ti Miming Sir, are you safe? We heard a noise. There is a man here who has broken his head open.

Zhao Dun I am safe, but tomorrow I shall not be safe. Tomorrow in the Golden Hall I shall impeach Tu'an Gu.

Music.

Zhao Dun Son of Heaven and father of my noble wife,
I come before you as a humble petitioner, fearful of your
displeasure, but anxious too for the good of the land.
A while ago it was your habit to listen to many voices for
advice. Now, those voices have been silenced, and you no
longer even attend the morning levee. Good men have left
the Court in despair, and one minister alone has your ear.
It is a situation that invites abuse.

Tu'an Gu Zhao Dun has insulted me before the whole
Court.

Zhao Dun And, sure enough, the signs of abuse are here.
In the Peach Garden yesterday you treated your loyal
subjects as targets of opportunity. But the poor have
sufferings enough without being made into objects of
sport. Then last night the body of an armed man was
found in my garden. He was Chu Ni, well known as a
servant and associate of Tu'an Gu. Clearly there had been
some plot.

Tu'an Gu This is outrageous. A man is found dead and
I am accused of plotting. How did this man die?

Zhao Dun By his own hand. He dashed his brains out
against a pagoda tree.

General laughter.

Emperor How very amusing. How many people would
have thought of that? But I do not understand, my dear
son-in-law, why this strange suicide should be blamed on
my loyal minister Tu'an Gu.

Tu'an Gu Sir, if there is treachery at Court, I have a
remedy. You may recall the Demon Mastiff you were sent

as a gift by the people of Tibet. Such dogs are said to sniff out treachery and deceit. Let my servants bring the dog here, and we shall see where danger and deception lie.

Emperor Splendid. Let the Demon Mastiff be brought.

Zhao Dun I have nothing to fear. My loyalty has never been questioned.

Sounds of cages being unlocked. Eunuchs bring on the Mastiff.

Tu'an Gu Go on, boy. Fetch out the traitor! Fetch!

The Mastiff is released. It makes straight for Zhao Dun's purple robe.

Now who is the traitor here, Zhao Dun?

Zhao Dun Help me, Ti Miming, help me!

Ti Miming Let him go, hell-hound, let him go! Now, master, flee. I will hold them back as long as I can.

Ti Miming kills the Demon Mastiff, and fights off Zhao Dun's pursuers, but eventually he is caught.

Tu'an Gu Zhao Dun is a traitor. Don't let him escape. Kill him. Massacre every member of his clan.

SCENE SIX
THE SLAUGHTER OF THE ZHAO CLAN

Zhao Dun I am Zhao Dun, now lord of a doomed clan. Your Royal Highness, my dear wife, listen to what I have to tell you now. My enemies are closing in on me and these may be my last words. You are carrying my child, my first-born. If it is a girl, no harm will come to it. But if it is a boy, let it be called the Orphan of Zhao. Hide my son well, I beg you, keep him safe. When he becomes a man, he will avenge his father's death.

Princess Do not speak of death. I cannot bear it.

Messenger Here is the gate of his house.

Zhao Dun, Zhao Dun, kneel now and hear the orders of the Emperor. 'Your family are traitors every one of them, and every one of them has been put to the sword. Your father is dead. Your uncles are dead. All your menfolk are dead. You alone have been spared, because you are married to our daughter and we could not have handed you over to the public executioner. Instead we will offer you the three imperial punishments. Choose one, therefore, and die. Thenceforth the Princess will be kept prisoner in this palace, entirely cut off from our family.'

Step forward now and choose. Poison, dagger or the bowstring. This is the Emperor's solemn decree, not to be delayed or disobeyed. Decide now and act.

Zhao Dun My wife, my wife, what is there to be done? I was loyal to the Emperor and it has all come to nothing. The traitor Tu'an Gu lies curled like a maggot, nibbling at the heart of the state. He holds all the power.

Princess May the Gods have pity on us. He is so cruel – we shall die and we shall lie unburied.

Zhao Dun We shall never be laid to rest in the tombs of our ancestors. But remember well what I told you, Your Royal Highness.

Princess I shall remember everything.

Zhao Dun My tears flow like rain. I go to another world, another sorrow.

He stabs himself.

Princess My dying lord, my breaking heart.

Messenger Zhao Dun has killed himself with the dagger. Let the Princess be locked in the Palace. I shall go back and report all this to my lord.

SCENE SEVEN
DOCTOR CHENG SAVES A CHILD

Cheng Ying I am Cheng Ying, a simple country doctor. Most of my life has been spent on the hillside, gathering herbs and roots for my medicine chest, and in my village tending the sick. Who would have thought that I should be summoned to the city, to deliver the first-born child of the Princess? Have they no doctors of their own, no servants of their clan? Yet here I stand, a nobody at the Palace gate.

Guard What are you? A pedlar?

Cheng Ying I am a country doctor, summoned to the bedside of the Princess.

Guard Why would the Princess choose an ignorant bumpkin like you?

Cheng Ying I have no idea. All I know is that I was summoned to the city and told to report to the Palace gate.

Guard . . . Unless, of course, they had already executed all the doctors of the household, for fear of treachery.

Cheng Ying Nobody in his right mind would think of executing all the doctors. It makes no sense.

Guard Look up.

Cheng Ying sees the heads of the executed family and servants.

The city has four gates, and every gate is decorated like this. Good luck with the Princess. When you've delivered the baby, no doubt they will find a reason for delivering your head to me, and I shall hang it . . . let me see . . . over there. It'll keep the crows happy. The Princess's Palace is on the right.

Maid You are the doctor? Come quickly.

Cheng Ying Is the Princess already in labour?

Maid You will see for yourself. She is grieving terribly. She has been groaning all night.

Cheng Ying Your Royal Highness, I am Cheng Ying, the doctor you sent for. You must permit me to place my hands upon your wrist.

Princess Oh, oh.

Cheng Ying What is this?

A cushion falls out from the Princess's robe.

I do not understand. You are not pregnant. You are mocking me for my simple country ways.

Princess Cheng Ying, I am not mocking you. Last night I gave birth to the Orphan of Zhao, and when I groan it is to cover his cries. Now you must think of a way to hide this baby and smuggle him away, so that later, when he becomes a man, he can have his revenge on the enemy of the Zhaos.

Cheng Ying Princess, Princess, now I understand. For the gates of the city are hung with this order: 'If anyone tries to steal the Orphan of Zhao, his whole family will be decapitated. None of his relations will be left alive.'

Princess Cheng Ying, I am a princess, and here I kneel to you. Three hundred souls are vested in this one child. He is the last of the Zhao clan. Have pity on him.

Cheng Ying What can I do? Already I am terribly afraid.

Princess (*to the Maid*) Take the child and give him to the doctor. Cheng Ying, I beg you save my son. I shall remember your name for ever.

Cheng Ying If I save your son, you must forget my name.

Forget my name, Princess, forget my family, my village, my prefecture. I myself no longer seem to know who I am, or why I have been chosen to save the Orphan of Zhao. If I do what the Princess asks, I shall lose everything.

SCENE EIGHT
THE ESCAPE FROM THE CITY

Han Jue I am General Han Jue and I serve the minister Tu'an Gu. He has sent me to watch the gates of the Princess's Palace, to make sure nobody leaves without being searched. He is afraid that the Princess has had a baby and that someone will try to smuggle it out. If anyone is found sheltering the Orphan of Zhao, he is to be decapitated, and his family wiped out, to the ninth generation. So, Captain, keep that gate secure.

Tu'an Gu, damn you, Tu'an Gu. When will we see the last of people like you? We had a strong state, once. Others were fighting among themselves. We were secure, or so we thought. Then you come along. You take the loyal sons of the Court, and chop off their heads in the marketplace. You sink your claws and teeth into the Court itself, and anyone who puts up a fight is eliminated. One by one they go. Tu'an Gu, damn you, Tu'an Gu.

Captain, I say, keep that gate secure. Bring me that man with the medicine chest in his arms. Who are you?

Cheng Ying I am a travelling doctor and my name is Cheng Ying.

Han Jue Where are you coming from?

Cheng Ying I've been brewing herbs and roots and administering medicines in the Princess's Palace.

Han Jue What do you have in that chest?

Cheng Ying Only herbs.

Han Jue What kind of herbs?

Cheng Ying Bellflower, licorice and peppermint.

Han Jue And might there be anything hidden in between?

Cheng Ying There is nothing hidden in between.

Han Jue Go!

Cheng Ying, come back! When I tell you to go, you are off like an arrow from a string. But when I call you back, it's like pulling hair over felt. Cheng Ying, Cheng Ying, you are hiding something – you are hiding unicorn seed. Move back, Captain – move away. This is not for you.

Guard I obey.

Cheng Ying, at a sign from Han Jue, opens the chest.

Han Jue Cheng Ying, you said you only had bellflower, licorice and peppermint. But I see a little root shaped like a child. I have found ginseng.

So this is the Orphan of Zhao, his forehead covered with tiny beads of sweat, and at the corner of his mouth – the froth of his mother's milk. He opens wide his sparkling eyes. He recognises me! How come you recognise me, lying here among the peppermint, quiet in your little box? Swallowing your voice. All tightly wrapped in your swaddling bands, so you can't move a tiny limb.

Cheng Ying, if I were to take this little bundle and hand it over, I would live in wealth and honour for the rest of my life. Excepting that they would say: he destroyed others for his own profit. And who would be left to avenge this everlasting wrong? Three hundred dead and only this baby survives, cradled in licorice.

And if Tu'an Gu finds you, he'll take you, skin, tendons and all, and chop you up into a nice meaty paste. Yes, he will, won't he! Yes, he will.

Cheng Ying, take this child and be on your way. If Tu'an Gu asks, I'll answer for it.

Cheng Ying Thank you, General.

Makes as if to walk out with the chest. Then turns back and kneels down.

Han Jue Cheng Ying, I told you, you are free to go. You think I am playing with you. Get out of here now.

Cheng Ying Thank you, General.

Again he makes as if to go, but returns and kneels.

Han Jue Cheng Ying, why have you come back yet again?

Cheng Ying General, if I get out of here with the baby, and you tell Tu'an Gu, he will send another general after me to arrest me. There's no way the Orphan can survive. So be it. General, arrest me and claim your reward. I will lay down my life with the Orphan.

Han Jue You think I am tricking you. I am not tricking you. Why should I let you go, only to send out the troops to go after you?

But your determination comes as a reproach to me. If you can be loyal, I can be loyal too. If you can be ready to die, I too should be ready to die. Take the child and keep him well hidden in the furthest reaches of the mountains. Teach him the arts of war and peace. Train him and, when he reaches manhood, tell him who he is. Tell him, when he takes his revenge, not to forget us, those who have died for him.

Slits his throat.

Cheng Ying Han Jue has slit his throat. He has made my decision for me. Now I must flee.

SCENE NINE
THE ESCAPE IS DISCOVERED

Tu'an Gu One of my eunuchs informed me: a baby was heard crying last night in the Princess's Palace. I had the place thoroughly searched. Nothing was found. Either the Princess has miscarried, or the baby has been smuggled out. Guard!

Guard My lord.

Tu'an Gu Tell General Han that I wish to speak with him.

Guard I will, sir, at once.

Goes inside. Comes out after a pause.

My lord, it is too late. General Han is dead. He has cut his throat.

Tu'an Gu A soldier does not do such a thing without good reason. There was a baby. The baby is gone. General Han is dead. Someone has defied me. Someone has rescued the Orphan of Zhao. There is only one thing to do. Messenger, go and proclaim throughout the city, throughout the whole land, that the baby must be returned to the Court. If not, then every male child born this last month will be put to the sword. There will be no pity.

SCENE TEN
AN EPISODE OF STERLING DEVOTION

Wife So many days my husband, Cheng Ying, has been gone. It makes me afraid. Normally he travels here in the mountains, and sometimes he will be delayed when the snow has blocked one of the passes, or when in spring a river is in spate. All I know is he was called to the city.

Then rumours began. They speak of the fall of a minister, the massacre of a clan. I know nothing of this. My husband knows nothing of such affairs. He is a humble man. Why should I feel such a weight of foreboding?

I look at our child, asleep in his cradle. Sometimes he seems to be dreaming; his tiny brow is wrinkled, and he cries ever so softly, as if in the distance. I place my little finger gently across the palm of his hand, and he grasps my finger as if he had seen fear in a dream. How strong his little grasp has become, in these few days. How strong his little fears have become.

First Neighbour Be careful for your child.

Wife Why do you say that?

Second Neighbour There's a storm brewing.

Wife I see no cloud in the sky.

Third Neighbour Better to keep that child indoors.

Fourth Neighbour Where is Cheng Ying? Still gone?

Fifth Neighbour Did he tell you when to expect him?

Sixth Neighbour Just keep that child well out of sight.

Wife All my neighbours run away, as if they were afraid to stay near me. They are afraid, but they will not tell me why.

Cheng Ying My dear wife. You are safe. Where is our child?

Wife Here. I hid him in the grain bin. Everyone is telling me to keep him out of sight. What's happening?

Cheng Ying They are killing all the Zhao clan.

Wife What is that to us? We have no connection with the Zhao clan.

Cheng Ying Look at this bundle that was entrusted to me. This is the last of the clan, the Orphan of Zhao. His mother the Princess begged me to take care of him.

Wife But you said no.

Cheng Ying How could I say no?

Wife She has wished a disaster upon us.

Cheng Ying She begged me to smuggle her child out of the city.

Wife She has put a curse upon us.

Cheng Ying I undertook to save her child. And General Han Jue killed himself, after letting us escape.

Wife It is a child of destruction, a massacre child, a child of revenge. I cannot bear to look at it.

Cheng Ying It is crying. It is hungry.

Wife I am not a wet-nurse. I have no milk for this child. Why did you bring this misfortune to this house?

Cheng Ying I have given my word. I must protect the child. And yet Tu'an Gu has said that if the Orphan of Zhao is not given up to be killed, then every new-born boy in the land will be slaughtered.

Wife They said a storm was brewing, and they looked at me in fear, as if they expected lightning to strike our house. You must give up the Orphan of Zhao at once. You must take him back. Take him back to the Princess. Tell her to look after her own child. We are poor. We have nothing. We have no soldiers to protect us. Why does she hate us like this?

Cheng Ying Look at our child. And look at this one. It is strange. They could be twins.

Wife But they are not twins. They are not. What are you thinking of?

Cheng Ying I said I would save the Orphan of Zhao. If I do so, our only child will undoubtedly be killed. He is known to all our neighbours. There are no secrets here for long.

Wife So you must not try to save the Orphan of Zhao. It is impossible.

Cheng Ying One way might be possible. If I could pass our child off as the Orphan . . .

Wife I do not believe I am hearing this from a father's lips.

Cheng Ying I cannot believe that I am saying these things. And yet I am. This child is the last of his clan. His father was killed by Tu'an Gu along with three hundred of their family and retainers. One poor soul alone survives. He must be given a chance to grow, so that justice can finally be done.

Wife What you call justice for his clan is murder for me.

Cheng Ying I will go visit Gongsun Chujiu. In his time he was a wise and upright minister. Maybe he will have some advice.

SCENE ELEVEN
THE MOUNTAIN RETREAT

Gongsun Chujiu A thatched cottage, a few acres, and a hoe – this is what my life has settled down to. Once I was Gongsun Chujiu, Grandee of the Second Order at the Court of the Emperor. But after the Peach Garden massacre I saw the way things were going. I saw how Tu'an Gu was grabbing all the power for himself, and I thought: I am too old for this. I left the Court and went back to farming. I live in Great Peace Village. At night I crawl inside the bed curtains and listen to the breathing of the cattle in the field. Now here I am, leaning on a brushwood gate, counting the lines of geese overhead.

Cheng Ying I'd better leave my burden here for a while, under this little cucumber trellis. Young master, I shall come back to look after you just as soon as I have talked with Gongsun Chujiu.

(*To the Servant.*) Please tell your lord that Cheng Ying is here and would like to speak with him.

Servant The doctor, Cheng Ying, is at the gate.

Gongsun Chujiu Invite him in. Cheng Ying, what brings you here?

Cheng Ying We are told to expect a storm.

Gongsun Chujiu You mean there are dark clouds over the city, over the Court. Yes, I have heard that. My old friend Zhao Dun has lost his life, and they say his whole clan has been exterminated. It is, well, remarkable. Remarkable.

Cheng Ying I see you are well informed.

Gongsun Chujiu I would not describe myself as well informed. (Let us walk in the garden.) For instance, I have also been told that General Han Jue, a good man, committed suicide. But I do not know why such a man would do this. There would have been a reason, of course. There would have to have been a good reason.

Cheng Ying If the General had been ordered to guard the Palace gate, for instance, for fear that a new-born child might be smuggled out, and if his conscience had told him to disobey his orders – something that went against the grain with him – he might have chosen death as a way of reconciling himself –

Gongsun Chujiu – to the escape of the Orphan of Zhao?

Cheng Ying I see that you really are well informed.

Gongsun Chujiu People tell me things. I don't know why, but when unusual events transpire, they seem to feel the urge to come and tell me, as you yourself have come all this way, with your medicine chest. Which I think I saw you place, rather carefully, under that little cucumber trellis over there.

Cheng Ying My lord, I am at your mercy. The Orphan of Zhao is at your mercy.

Gongsun Chujiu You chose well, when you chose this place of trust. Bring the child to me. Take care not to frighten him. Bring him indoors.

Cheng Ying Find a way to pity us and save this Orphan and save the other infants in the land.

Gongsun Chujiu You are risking your life.

Cheng Ying I expect to be killed as soon as they track me down. I expect my child to be killed with me. But I made an undertaking to save this infant. My own boy is of the same age. And it seemed to me that I could go back to the Court with my own son, and tell Tu'an Gu that this was the Orphan of Zhao. He would kill us both in an instant. But he is going to kill us either way. Of that I am sure. This way, at least, I save the lives of all the other infant boys. Meanwhile I trust you to keep the Orphan safe.

Gongsun Chujiu It is a remarkable plan. How old are you, Cheng Ying?

Cheng Ying I'm nearly forty-five.

Gongsun Chujiu This child will have to be twenty before he takes revenge for his clan. With another twenty years, you'll only be sixty-five, but I shall be ninety. I'll most likely be dead. Cheng Ying, if you are willing to give up your child, hand him over to me. Then go to Tu'an Gu and tell him that I am sheltering the Orphan of Zhao in

Great Peace Village. He will kill us both. Your task will be to bring up the Orphan of Zhao, and prepare him for his revenge.

Cheng Ying, do as I say. I am an old man. I will not last through these evening drums and morning bells. I am a man of seventy and death is nothing out of the ordinary. It makes no difference when it comes.

SCENE TWELVE
THE SUBSTITUTION OF THE CHILD

Wife (*sings*)
The dragon on his tile,
The monster in the deep,
The panther in the pagoda tree –
They all curl up and sleep.

And as they sleep they snore
And as they snore they smile –
The panther in the pagoda tree,
The dragon on his tile.

The baby in his crib
Is laughing in his sleep,
The panther in the pagoda tree
Is smiling on
The dragon tile
And the monster in the deep,
My love,
The monster in the deep.

Ah!

Cheng Ying We startled you.

Wife I am ashamed. I was not expecting a visitor. I am not properly dressed. And besides, you both look at me in a strange way, as if I were much to be pitied. Who is this noble gentleman?

Cheng Ying This is Gongsun Chujiu. He has come with me to ask you to make a great sacrifice.

Wife No. No!

Gongsun Chujiu It is true that you are much to be pitied. We are all to be pitied, but you are the more to be pitied. When Tu'an Gu realises, as he by now must realise, that the Orphan of Zhao has escaped, he will seek out your husband and kill him and your son, and maybe you yourself.

Wife Give him the Orphan of Zhao. What can we do if the most powerful man in the land has decided the Orphan must die? We are nothing. The Orphan is nothing to us, the heir to a clan which has disappeared. Let him kill this Orphan and be done with it.

Cheng Ying I cannot hand over the Orphan. I made an undertaking. I did not realise quite what it would cost, but I knew it would cost me dear. When they come for me, I know I can face death. But I cannot face the shame of having betrayed the Orphan of Zhao.

Wife You are ashamed to betray this stranger's child. But your own son – your own child you *can* betray. What sort of father is that?

Cheng Ying I am a man in a trap. I made an undertaking. I see now it will cost me everything.

Gongsun Chujiu It is a noble sacrifice he makes. Give me the child. See how I kneel to you.

Wife You are an old man, and a nobleman too. You must not kneel to me. The sight of it revolts me, as if the world were turned inside out. Get back on your feet, old man.

Gongsun Chujiu Look, I prostrate myself.

Wife I never asked you to demean yourself like this. My child will die. I can see that. I cannot understand why, but I can see that it will happen. I am a woman, and there is nothing in the end that I can do.

Gongsun Chujiu My daughter.

Wife (*handing over the child*) What kind of man is that? He calls me daughter as he kills me.

SCENE THIRTEEN
THE INTERROGATION OF THE MAID

Tu'an Gu A baby's voice was heard. And now there is no baby and no voice in the night. What has happened to the Orphan of Zhao?

Maid There is no Orphan of Zhao. There never was. The baby was stillborn. The voice your spy heard must have been the weeping Princess. She was distraught. I thought she was going to kill herself. She could not bear the sight of her dead child. She told me to take it at once and throw it in the river.

Tu'an Gu That would be very convenient if it were true. But you are lying to me. You knew that I would be pleased to be told the child was dead. Why did you not show it to me?

Maid My mistress was beside herself. I was afraid she would go quite mad. She told me to throw it in the river. It was a poor misshapen thing – one of the mistakes of nature. I threw it away with the afterbirth, and washed myself to be rid of it.

Guard Sir, there is a man at the gate who claims to have found the Orphan of Zhao.

Tu'an Gu Now we will learn about your lies. Show the man in.

Guard This is him.

Tu'an Gu Come inside.

Cheng Ying performs greeting rituals.

Cheng Ying This humble person is the travelling physician, Cheng Ying.

Tu'an Gu Where is the Orphan of Zhao?

Cheng Ying He is hidden in Great Peace Village in the house of Gongsun Chujiu.

Tu'an Gu How do you know?

Cheng Ying I travel for my work, and I happen to know Gongsun Chujiu. I went to visit him and saw a baby in the bedroom, lying on an embroidered cushion and wrapped in a fine brocade. I thought: 'Gongsun Chujiu is a man of seventy. He never had a son or daughter. Where does this one come from?' And I said to him: 'This must be the Orphan of Zhao.' He turned pale at once, and didn't know what to say.

Maid You are lying, you traitor. The Orphan of Zhao is dead.

Cheng Ying I saw this baby and came to the city as fast as I could.

Tu'an Gu Why should a man like you, a nobody, denounce the noble Gongsun Chujiu? What motive could you have for coming and telling us this story? For if it is not true it will certainly cost you your life.

Maid He wants money. He's after a reward. I know him.

Cheng Ying I do not know you, or why you are insisting that the Orphan of Zhao is dead. I have a motive in this which is nothing to do with a reward. There is no enmity between Gongsun Chujiu and me. As Your Lordship rightly says, I am a nobody. I do not rise to the level of such enmities. But I have heard the proclamation that you want all the male infants in China rounded up and killed. So, first of all, I want to save them. Secondly, at forty-five, I have become the father of a boy who is not yet one month old. I should not dare to conceal him from your men, but if I handed him over I would be left without an heir. As I see it, if the Orphan of Zhao is found, the living souls of a whole state will be saved from harm, and my child too will be safe.

Maid Your child. Your child. What's the safety of your child to that of the Orphan of Zhao?

They realise the implication of her remark.

Tu'an Gu The woman has been lying all along. Kill her this minute.

The Soldiers kill the Maid.

Now, Cheng Ying, you understand what is at stake for you. Lead us to where the Orphan is hidden.

SCENE FOURTEEN
THE NOBLE DEATH OF GONGSUN CHUJIU

Gongsun Chujiu I am Gongsun Chujiu. Not long ago I talked with Cheng Ying about how to save the Orphan of Zhao. He went down to the city to denounce me. By this time, Tu'an Gu must be on his way. I can see a cloud of dust rising over the little bridge, and rows of lances and swords shimmering in the sun. I know that I shall die this very morning.

Tu'an Gu Soldiers, surround Great Peace Village. Cheng Ying! Which is the house of Gongsun Chujiu?

Cheng Ying It is this one.

Tu'an Gu Bring the old man over here. Gongsun Chujiu, do you know your crime?

Gongsun Chujiu I live in a quiet village in the mountains. I cultivate my garden. I am not aware of any crime.

Tu'an Gu I remember you well, old man. You were a friend and ally of Zhao Dun. And now you are hiding the Orphan of Zhao.

Gongsun Chujiu I am an old man. Do you think I have the heart of a bear, or the gall of a leopard? I wouldn't dare hide the Orphan you speak of.

Tu'an Gu No beating, no confession. Soldiers, pick a big club and give him a thrashing.

They beat him.

Gongsun Chujiu Who told you? Who informed on me? Whose tongue was the sword that will cut off my head?

Tu'an Gu Cheng Ying, here, informed on you.

Gongsun Chujiu The eagle rides the wind. Cheng Ying, I curse you. You are the wild wind to this far-striking eagle.

Tu'an Gu Where have you hidden the child, old man? Confess and spare yourself some torture.

Gongsun Chujiu What child do I have to hide? Who saw him?

Tu'an Gu So you won't confess? Soldiers, beat him soundly.

They beat him.

It seems he's going to be obstinate. Cheng Ying, you denounced him. You beat him for me.

Cheng Ying My lord, I am a travelling doctor. I'm hardly strong enough to go gathering herbs. How can I give him a beating?

Tu'an Gu Maybe he knows something about you. That's why you won't risk beating him.

Cheng Ying No. I'll beat him since you order me to.

Tu'an Gu I see you look through the clubs to choose something slender. Are you afraid he'll denounce you once the pain sets in?

Cheng Ying I will take a thick stick.

Tu'an Gu Wait a moment. First you picked a thin stick. Now you choose the thickest. Perhaps you think that if you beat him to death with two or three strokes, you won't run the risk of him implicating you.

Cheng Ying What am I supposed to do? If I take a thin stick, that isn't right. If I take a thick one, that isn't right either.

Tu'an Gu Just take a medium stick. Gongsun Chujiu, you foolish old man, do you realise that it's Cheng Ying who is beating you? Confess quickly.

Gongsun Chujiu I feel I've been beaten all day, but no stick has hurt me like this one. Cheng Ying, why are you beating me?

Cheng Ying Confess, you old fool, confess. Otherwise I'll have to beat you to death.

Gongsun Chujiu Allright, I'll confess. The two of us discussed how to save this child.

Tu'an Gu The two of you. Which two of you? Tell me the truth and I'll spare you your life.

Gongsun Chujiu If you want me to tell you who, I'll tell

33

you. I'll tell you who. Aiya! These words spring to my lips. Now I must swallow them.

Tu'an Gu Cheng Ying, are you part of this?

Cheng Ying Don't you try fingering me, old man. Don't you try fingering me.

Tu'an Gu You said the two of you discussed how to save the child.

Gongsun Chujiu I didn't know what I was saying. I don't know up from down.

Soldier enters with child in arms.

Soldier Sir, we have discovered the Orphan of Zhao, hidden in a hole in the ground.

Tu'an Gu Bring him here. I shall chop him in three with my own hand.

One! Two! I shall hack this little seed of disaster in three.

Gongsun Chujiu I see Cheng Ying, his heart has been scalded with boiling oil, yet he must not shed a single tear in front of others. Cheng Ying's child is dead, and now it is my turn to die. Maybe our names will be remembered. And maybe one day revenge will come. For now, I have only one thing left to do.

He kills himself by dashing out his brains.

Soldier Gongsun Chujiu has dashed his head against the steps.

Tu'an Gu Ha! The Orphan is dead, and his protector too. Now we can let the matter rest.

Cheng Ying, I owe you thanks for what you have done today. And I was thinking – you told me you yourself have a son. You look startled. You recoil.

Cheng Ying I have a new-born son, yes.

Tu'an Gu You are luckier than me, my friend. I have no son, and now that I am fifty I doubt I ever will have. I'll make a deal with you. Bring your son to the Court, and let us share in his upbringing. Let me adopt your son.

Cheng Ying It is an honour and a great kindness that you propose, but his mother will grieve if she loses her son.

Tu'an Gu His mother is his mother, and always will be. As you will always be his father. You will conduct his education in the civil arts. And I shall train him in hunting and the arts of war. He will remain your son, but he will become my heir.

Cheng Ying Sir, we are simple country people, and my wife will be ashamed to come to the Court. You are too generous.

Tu'an Gu Cheng Ying, exceptional service deserves an exceptional reward. You delivered the Orphan into our hands. Now you deserve your reward.

SCENE FIFTEEN
THE SONG OF GENERAL WEI JIANG

Wei Jiang I am Wei Jiang. Eighteen years I have spent here on the border with my men, watching for any enemy attack, far from the Court, far from my home. I chose this long exile rather than remain in a city where Tu'an Gu ruled supreme, but it was a bitter choice, and life here is bitter for my men. We seldom receive visitors, for this is a military zone, and normally those who come here, come here to attack us. Their bones lie in white heaps at the foot of our bastions. They have joined the ranks of the unburied.

35

This morning, a guard spotted a young man making his way up the pass, as if coming from the city. His progress was slow, though he jumped from rock to rock as if born in the mountains. As he came closer, we could see that he was gathering herbs and roots, and taking a thousand diversions. He had the air of one happily absorbed in his work – a scholar, by his dress, doubtless a student of medicine. How little he seemed to care what dangers might await him on the other side of the hill. As evening was approaching, I sent some guards down to escort him to our camp.

Guard General, we have questioned the stranger. He carries an authorisation from the Court, permitting him to search for rare plants throughout this prefecture.

Wei Jiang Bring him to my presence. He must be a man of exceptional spirit. I think if we had not fetched him he would have spent the night on the cold mountainside.

Guard Prostrate yourself before the General.

Student My lord.

Wei Jiang You may rise. We have been watching you, leaping like a goat among the rocks.

Student General, I was excited to find so many rare specimens, plants that I have only read about in books, or seen on the apothecary's shelf. Suddenly the world lay open to me like a learned encyclopedia. The grasses are in flower and the ferns are putting out their spring shoots.

Wei Jiang Young man, if you had spent eighteen years living off those bitter fern-shoots, you might perhaps have been a little less excited. (*He pauses.*) Or did you mean something more than that? 'The ferns are putting out their spring shoots.'

Student You are General Wei Jiang, I think.

Wei Jiang I am.

Student I was entrusted with a message for you, should I have the good fortune to be brought into your presence.

Wei Jiang Excellent! Well? Give me the message.

The Student looks at the guards. The General signals for them to withdraw.

Student My message is that the Emperor is ill, and that there is no known cure for the growth that is killing him. The element of fire is rising in his liver and his heart. Perhaps he may last another month or two. The Emperor is brave in the face of death, and does not wish anyone to know of his condition. In consequence, the Court is not aware that His Majesty's sickness is anything more than the usual debility, after a life devoted to certain excesses.

Wei Jiang That is all?

Student That is all.

Wei Jiang And the identity of my informant?

Student One who wishes you nothing but good.

Wei Jiang Whoever that was, he chose you well. You have made a long journey, and a dangerous one. You have crossed – let me see – seven rivers in spate. You seem to have travelled alone. You are dressed as a student of medicine and, as you approached this camp, you treated us to an elegant piece of theatre – a young scholar, delighted to be out in the mountains, gathering herbs, without so much as a thought about where to lay his head come nightfall. Show me your treasures – open that chest. Now, my young medical student – what is this?

Student If only I knew – that is what excited me. It's a cress, of course, as you can see – the streams round here are full of it. It's like a miniature version of our watercress.

And yet the leaves are pointed – I've never seen it before. It is hot on the tongue, much hotter than any cress known to me. It must have powerful properties.

Wei Jiang And this?

Student It is the bulb of a lily – I nearly fell to my death gathering it from a crevasse – but I found seed too – I have great hopes for it.

Wei Jiang What colour is the flower?

Student I saw no flower. But, from the size of the old seed-heads I could tell it must be magnificent.

Wei Jiang Guards! Take this young man and feed him well. Find him a place to sleep. You will discover, my brave young scholar, that we live here as wise men recommend: 'Simple food, water, and the crook of your arm for a pillow.' Good night.

So the Emperor is dying, and my unknown well-wisher suggests that I move fast. If not, Tu'an Gu may soon make a move to usurp the throne.

Of course it could all be a trick. If I act now upon this intelligence, I may well put my life in danger. But if I do not act, danger may easily find me out, even here in this mountain obscurity. The choice is not hard to make.

Sings.

The moon is sharp on the blade.
The dew shines on the hill.
The heart bleeds dark
And my men lie still.

The heads on the palisades
Dried in the wind so black
Call out to the venturing foe:
Turn back, fool, turn back.

Here snores no feasted clown
Who has drunk disgrace with his wine.
Here drools no amorous dupe
In the lap of his concubine.

Here watches a bitter pride
In exile lonely and long.
He serves an unjust lord.
He endures a continuing wrong.

One watches. One endures
On the ramparts, on the towers,
The laughter of the stars,
The taunts of the small hours.

Who sweeps my ancestors' graves?
Who holds the reins for my son?
Will my dog still come to my call?
Does my wife sleep alone?

I serve an unjust lord.
Exile is an early tomb.
The heart bleeds dark.
Death is a journey home.

By the bright dew on the hill,
By the sharp blade of the moon,
I shall wake my grieving men.
I shall make that journey soon.

End of Part One.

Part Two

SCENE SIXTEEN
THE SONG OF THE GROOM

Ballad-Singer
It is seen that the loveliest girls have begun
To lower their eyes
And older men leave poems for you to find
Hinting in delicate images
At what is on their mind.
All this seems to come to you as a surprise.

Yesterday you were a child.
Today you are neither child nor man
But held as a petal held pivoting
On a gossamer thread,
Wanting no new love yet, no, nor wishing to give
More love than a child well can.

They watch you. They envy the young groom
As he hands you the reins
And helps you with exquisite modesty and tact,
Loving the child in you still, fearing the man,
Uncertain each day just how you may react.
You thank the groom for his pains.

He hands you the sealskin quiver,
The archer's ring and the glove.
He stretches the gut string taut and he proffers the bow
And he lowers his eyes and he trembles,
Fearing his fear will show.
For he dreads to betray his love.

Go forth, go ride to your sport.
Find your prey and show your skill.

Shoot from the saddle. Let your aim be true.
Only one man knows who you are,
How many heroes have died for you
And whose blood it is your fate to spill.
    Be on your way.
    Be a child for one more day.
One whom you love your blood dooms you to kill.

One whom you love your blood dooms you to kill.

SCENE SEVENTEEN
THE RETURN OF GENERAL WEI JIANG

Wei Jiang, accompanied by troops, comes back to the city. Cheng Ying, passing him on the street, tries to avoid him.

Wei Jiang Officer. Take hold of that man and bring him to me.

The Soldiers do so brutally. Cheng Ying prostrates himself before the General.

Eighteen years I have been gone from the city, but I recognised that traitor instantly – the way he scurried along the street, hugging the wall, like a dog from a whipping. I know you well, old man, and yet your name escapes me.

Cheng Ying I am Cheng Ying. Have mercy on me.

Wei Jiang Now I remember why I despise you. You were the traitor who betrayed Gongsun Chujiu.

Cheng Ying I do not know why you are saying this.

Wei Jiang 'I do not know why you are saying this.' I am saying this, dog, because – though eighteen years have passed since you denounced Gongsun – this is the first opportunity I have had to confront you. Luckily for you, the wars have kept me far from the city. But the report of your treachery – hold him fast! – travelled a long way. Let me whisper it in your ear. You betrayed my friend, that noble minister. You betrayed the Princess who entrusted her child to you. And you betrayed the Orphan of Zhao. How many more have you betrayed, or was that enough for you?

Cheng Ying I was only ever a simple doctor. I do not know this minister. I do not know this Orphan of Zhao. The name means nothing to me.

Wei Jiang Oh, it means nothing to you. Beat him till he remembers. Beat him for his treachery.

Cheng Ying Ah, ah!

Wei Jiang Beat him the way he beat the noble Gongsun Chujiu to death.

Cheng Ying No, wait. Wait a moment and hear me. It may be I deserve to die, but I have a secret which must not die with me.

Wei Jiang What secret, dog? Whisper your secret in my ear.

Cheng Ying The Orphan of Zhao is not dead.

Wei Jiang Liar. A child was found and killed. You denounced the minister and they ransacked his home. I took great care to learn the story from witnesses. I am not mistaken in this.

Cheng Ying A child was killed, yes, but the child who was killed was not the Orphan of Zhao. I of all people should know. That was my child. That was *my* child. My child.

Wei Jiang How do you expect me to believe this story?

Cheng Ying General Wei, you had better believe my story, because if you do not believe my story it is you who will endanger the life of the Orphan of Zhao. It is you who will betray him, not me.

General, you have come back to the capital after your long exile and your anger is written plainly on your brow. You are a bitter man. Your soldiers are bitter men. You have arrived in this city of eunuchs, covered with the dust of the road, and with a great righteous anger in your hearts.

No doubt you terrify all who encounter you. You terrify me, I freely admit it. But death does not terrify me. No, death is something I have longed for ever since the slaughter of my child. Go ahead and kill me. But be aware of this: the Orphan of Zhao does not yet know who he is. Gongsun knew, and he died to protect him. My wife knew, and her sorrows killed her many years ago. I am the last to know.

And there is something else I know, something that very few in this city are aware of. I know why you have come back here after so long. The Emperor is dying. I am his doctor. I have attended him these last years, and I know that he does not have long to live. And yet I have not thought it proper to inform his ministers.

Wei Jiang Someone took care to inform me. Why was I informed, and not his ministers?

Cheng Ying 'Someone' no doubt thought that even now, after all these years of corruption, there might still exist, somewhere in some far-flung corner of the empire, one righteous man. Somewhere beyond the mastiff's leash, the soldier's lance, the grasp of the eunuchs, there might still be found – like a rare cress growing in a stream, or a lily on a ledge in a crevasse – a hero with sufficient courage and humanity to stand up to Tu'an Gu and stop him

43

becoming Emperor. Everyone holds you to be a man of integrity, General. But what's the use of your integrity up there on the bare mountainside, when the real danger is here at the Court?

Wei Jiang How dare you talk to me like that?

Cheng Ying I told you I dare talk to you like that because I do not fear death.

Wei Jiang If this is all a lie, I shall find out soon enough, and it will be the worse for you. But if it is true, there is one thing you must do, and you must do it soon. The times are going to be dangerous, and none of us can tell which day will be his last. You must inform that young man of his story and his identity. If he is the Orphan of Zhao, he will certainly know where his duty lies. Tu'an Gu must finally be made to pay the price for his crimes. And I hear he has adopted a son . . .

Cheng Ying General Wei, don't think of touching his adopted son. If you kill Cheng Bo, you will be killing the Orphan of Zhao.

Wei Jiang takes a moment to understand this remark. Then he bursts out laughing.

So the serpent was raised in the bosom of the Court.

Cheng Ying It was the safest place. The noble Gongsun thought up the plan.

Wei Jiang And yet the plan was based upon the slaughter of your child.

Cheng Ying says nothing.

Doctor Cheng, I can see that I owe you an apology for the insults written on your suffering flesh. You seem to be a man born to great and unexpected sacrifices. Tell me one thing: when shall I be permitted to meet this Orphan of Zhao?

Cheng Ying You have met him already.

Wei Jiang Ah!

Cheng Ying You thought of killing him, as you thought of killing me just now. But I was always confident that his honesty would impress you.

Wei Jiang His honesty and his spirit. He came up the valley, leaping from rock to rock, like a goat or some kind of mountain deer. And we watched him in surprise, for we were quite unaccustomed to visitors, and the ground he was dancing through was known to us as a battlefield. We had fought for every bog and every stream of it, year after year. We had heard the groans of our wounded companions all through the long nights, and we had watched the dawn break on their sightless faces. And now came this young man. What had been a place of torment to us seemed a garden to him. The world, he said, lay open to him like an encyclopedia.

So this was the son of my childhood friend, Zhao Dun. No wonder my first thought was to give him shelter.

Well, well – it was worth a long exile – to return to this!

SCENE EIGHTEEN
CHENG BO

Cheng Bo I am Cheng Bo, son of Cheng Ying, the Emperor's physician. I live at home in the imperial city, and study medicine in the evenings with my natural father. But I have another father by adoption. The noble lord, the Chief Minister, Tu'an Gu, long ago named me as his adopted son. From him by day I learn the arts of hunting and war. He has taught me to ride and to hunt in the imperial parks.

45

I have shared my life harmoniously with my two fathers, and I love them both, but recently Cheng Ying entrusted me with a great secret. The Emperor is dying, and does not wish the Court to know it. Even my adopted father Tu'an Gu, the Emperor, was to be kept in the dark. I do not know why this should be.

To ease the Emperor in his final sickness, my father sent me to gather a rare plant in a distant province. There too I was to seek out General Wei Jiang and tell him of the Emperor's condition. No one was to know that I was carrying this message. It was the first time that I had borne such a responsibility, and I was keen to win my father's praise.

I had never been alone before, still less undertaken such a journey.

The first town I came to had been set alight, and the granaries were still smouldering.

Peasant You see how pitiless they are. They have destroyed the seed-corn. We shall all die of famine. It is inevitable.

Cheng Bo Who has done this? Who has attacked the town?

Peasant The tax inspectors have attacked the town. Who else would have done this?

Cheng Bo Does the government burn the people's grain?

Peasant Friends, there's a young scholar here with a question: Does the government burn the people's grain?

General laughter.

Cheng Bo In the second town, the officers were conducting a recruitment drive from house to house. I saw a man who had severed his own hand rather than be taken off to fight in the war. In the third town they were putting down a rebellion. The victims of torture were displayed in the streets, their faces set in expressions of inconceivable hatred.

After that I met with misery all along the road. I heard the Emperor's name cursed and my own adopted father spoken of in a language I had never encountered. I was angry to witness these bitter insults, and wanted to defend Tu'an Gu's honour. But I kept my counsel and listened to the same tale of suffering and abuse every morning in the market, and every night beside the tavern fire.

But I have known the Emperor all my life. He is a good old man. And I love my adoptive father. How could I reconcile what I was hearing and seeing with what I knew of their virtues? I went on towards the war zone, puzzled and saddened. I told myself that these abuses could not be sanctioned by the Emperor, or by Tu'an Gu. It must be that they were unaware of the things being done in their name.

An order is given – say, for a new tax. It is passed from hand to hand, from mouth to mouth, and at each stage somebody seeks to profit from it, so that what began as a reasonable tax ends up as a monstrous imposition. The money is collected – it is extorted brutally from the people. Then it is passed back along the chain. At each stage again, a deduction is made by the interested parties, so that what finds its way into the imperial coffers is exactly what was asked for – no more, no less.

In that case, it could be that neither the Emperor nor my father Tu'an Gu was aware of what was being done in his name. Someone had to inform them of these terrible abuses. I could tell my adopted father, and Tu'an Gu – if there was time – could broach the matter with the Emperor.

This thought made me happy for a while, until I remembered that, because of the secrecy demanded by the Emperor, I could not inform Tu'an Gu about my long journey. All he knew was that I had been pursuing my studies. How could I tell him of all the cruel scenes I had witnessed? How could I say that I had crossed the war zone and come to the very frontier of the kingdom, and that I had heard the Emperor everywhere reviled, and his own name cursed?

At the very least, I thought next, when I get home, I will tell my natural father, Cheng Ying, about my theory that dreadful abuses in the kingdom are being committed by lower ministers and governors in the name of the Emperor and Tu'an Gu. And I will ask Cheng Ying's advice.

But when I thought of how this conversation would go, a strange new fear overwhelmed me. I asked myself what I would do if Cheng Ying listened to my experiences and shook his head at my theory, if he told me that Tu'an Gu had informants in every city, in every village, and knew precisely what was done in his name. What would I do then? How would I face my second father with this knowledge in my heart?

My second father! When had I ever called him that? Surely I had always loved him as much as I loved Cheng Ying. Surely I had always been open with both of them. How had this conflict suddenly entered my life?

I walked on towards the frontier, up through the deserted valleys filled with flowers that I had never before seen. And when I met soldiers on the road they spoke not of the Emperor or Tu'an Gu, but only of General Wei Jiang – a man they seemed to revere. I felt as though I had crossed into a new country, where the beauty of the hillside was in harmony with the justice of the ruler.

I knew of course that I was on a mission. But the meaning of this mission, and my father's purpose in sending me – that was something I felt I was still too young to inquire. I found the rare plant that my father had sent me for – the plant that would make a salve for the dying Emperor. By then I knew that Wei Jiang and his men were watching me. The soldiers called out to me and their voices were friendly. I climbed the last few feet, and they escorted me up to the General's camp.

SCENE NINETEEN
THE SHOOTING OF THE GEESE

Tu'an Gu I am Tu'an Gu, Chief Minister to the Emperor. Who knows? Maybe before too long I shall be Emperor myself. The old man is certainly no longer what he was – his dissipations are at last catching up with him, and I do not expect he has many years, or even many months more to live. His doctor, my friend Cheng Ying, has promised to tell me as soon as he appears to be dying, so that I can make my move. I have waited long and patiently for this moment, and I do not intend to be thwarted in my plan. I want the Empire for myself and for my son – my son who, every day, is proving himself worthy to become a prince. A little innocent, perhaps, for he has led a sheltered life, but a strong spirit and already a skilled hunter.

Cheng Bo Look, Father, the geese.

Cheng Bo shoots an arrow at a formation of geese flying overhead.

Tu'an Gu One shot brought down two geese. It is an omen.

Cheng Bo They must have landed in the Forbidden Palace. Now I shall never find them.

Tu'an Gu How so?

Cheng Bo You have always told me never to venture within its grounds.

Tu'an Gu It seems that you were destined to go in there. But I shall wait for you here at the gate.

Cheng Bo Why, Father?

Tu'an Gu Just do as I say. Go in there, retrieve your trophies, come straight back to me here.

Cheng Bo He is angry with me, and yet he does not wish to show it. I wonder why.

Tu'an Gu He will meet that mad old woman and she will denounce me. But why worry? He shot two geese with one arrow, and that is a rare omen. Maybe the Emperor will die soon, and I shall need the boy's help. The old general, Wei Jiang, is back in the city, suddenly returned from the frontier. He is my enemy. But the boy shot *two* geese. I have no other enemy. Who else is left?

Cheng Bo enters the Forbidden Palace.

Cheng Bo This must have been a garden once. Nobody has swept the leaves for years. The steps and the pathways are quite obscured under them. Thorny weeds have sprung up everywhere. The pavilions have collapsed and their cinnabar columns are strewn about the lakeside. The bright roof-tiles lie almost concealed in the moss. Kingfishers skim the surface of the water, and troupes of gibbons pass noisily overhead.

Here are the two geese, transfixed by a single arrow. What did I ever do to earn such luck? Or is it not luck but a destiny no one has yet explained to me?

Guard Hey, you. Nobody is allowed to enter here. What are you doing?

Cheng Bo My father the Chief Minister gave me permission to retrieve two geese I had shot.

Guard Oh, your father gave you permission! And what is your father's name if I may ask?

Cheng Bo Tu'an Gu. And, guard, if you do not believe me, you can ask him yourself. He is waiting at the outer gate.

Guard Oh, your father is waiting at the outer gate, is he? And I suppose the Emperor and all his eunuchs are with him?

Goes to look. Comes back and prostrates himself.

Oh, my lord, forgive me. My orders are to guard the Princess.

Cheng Bo What princess lives here? I know of no such princess.

Guard I spoke out of turn. Please, master, do not tell your father what I said.

Princess Who is this young man who dares defy the orders of the Emperor?

Guard He is the son of the noble Chief Minister Tu'an Gu.

Princess That is strange. I was unaware that Tu'an Gu had ever had a son. But *I* had a son until Tuan Gu hunted the baby down. And this young man looks just as I imagine my son would have looked had he not been betrayed. He could be my son. He *is* my son and I am doomed to weep for him. Day by day, night by night, I must weep here in this prison for the ghost of my slaughtered son.

Cheng Bo Who are you, Princess? And why do you live here in this desolate pavilion?

Princess Go ask your father who I am, and why I live here in this monkey palace. Ask him who he is. Ask him who you are. Go ask the geese in the sky. Go ask the gibbons shrieking in the treetops. Can a monkey keep a secret? Can a dog betray a minister? Can a great crime lie unavenged? You call yourself that man's son, but your face torments me with a thousand recollections. Go away at once, young man. You are not who you say you are. Torment me no further.

Cheng Bo I shall obey you.

Cheng Bo returns to the garden gate.

Tu'an Gu You are shaken. What happened? What did you see?

Cheng Bo Only a roofless palace full of monkeys. It was nothing.

Tu'an Gu Did anyone speak to you?

Cheng Bo I told you. There was nobody there.

Tu'an Gu He is lying. My son is lying. For the first time he is keeping a secret from me.

SCENE TWENTY
THE EMPEROR AND THE GENERAL

Wei Jiang You summoned me in secret.

Emperor I heard you had come back to the city after all these years, and that reminded me of something that troubled me.

Wei Jiang I cannot guess what troubled you.

Emperor Even this sentence of yours sounds like a rebuke. You rebuked me many years ago, and I shrugged it off at the time. I was a young man and did many foolish things.

But I am dying now, and perhaps it is not too late to make some sort of amends. It is strange, isn't it, how certain rebukes lodge in the memory while others simply – simply evaporate. I am criticised all the time here in the Court. They tell me I am a drunkard. Well, yes. Who isn't? That's really not a matter of consequence. But you rebuked me by turning your back on me. You had been one of my closest advisers – and then, it seemed, you could no longer bear the sight of me. For some reason, that lodged in the mind.

Wei Jiang You forget. You had a favourite. I could not breathe the same air as Tu'an Gu. That is why I had to turn my back on you. But I was loyal. I have spent long years defending the empire.

Emperor Yes, you were loyal. I appreciate that. And you were always honest with me. So now tell me. What made you return, unannounced, to the city?

Wei Jiang I was told you were dying.

Emperor You were told. I see. And – let me guess – you thought Tu'an Gu would make a move for the throne.

Wei Jiang It would be in character, yes.

Emperor What would happen then?

Wei Jiang Tu'an Gu is universally detested. Nobody would stand for it. There would be a rebellion. His house and yours would be marked for oblivion. Your tomb, if you were lucky enough to be buried at all, would suffer the same fate as the graves of the Zhao clan. Everything would be obliterated. The people would be very angry.

Emperor Zhao Dun was a traitor and suffered a traitor's fate. Was that not just?

Wei Jiang Not on the evidence of a dog. You were a foolish young man, and you were tricked by a wily minister and a well-trained dog.

Emperor You do not waste words. I am afraid for my family.

Wei Jiang You do right to be afraid for your family and for the tombs of your ancestors. You yourself have set the precedent in this.

Emperor What shall I do? My life is slipping away.

Wei Jiang Give me your royal seal as a sign. I shall speak to the Palace Guard.

Emperor What shall I say to Tu'an Gu?

Wei Jiang Say nothing. Do not admit him to your presence tonight. By dawn I shall have everything under control and it will be too late. Are you afraid of dying?

Emperor I am afraid of making a bad death.

Wei Jiang Do not be afraid. Wisdom is strength, and you are at last becoming wise.

Emperor Go, take my seal. Be wise on my behalf.

SCENE TWENTY-ONE
THE PAINTING OF THE SCROLL

Cheng Ying Wei Jiang was right. I must tell Cheng Bo his whole history. But how shall I begin? How to break the news to him that he is not my son, that I am not his father? How to say I lied to you? I taught you always to be truthful, but, forgive me, I lied to you in this one small matter?

Ghost of Gongsun Don't forget I have a say in this.

Cheng Ying Gongsun Chujiu! What are you doing out there in the rain?

Ghost of Gongsun Planting cucumbers. I made a little trellis of bamboo, and I tied the young vines gently to the trellis, so they could learn to cling to the bamboo and hold the cucumbers off the ground. But when I looked under the trellis, I saw a little baby laughing through the cucumber leaves, and pulling all the flowers off the vines. And somehow I knew that this mischievous little baby was my death. My death was laughing at me and waving its chubby little limbs and simply asking to be picked up. So I reached forward and embraced the baby, and that was a difficult embrace. But I have no regrets. Only, I *would* regret it – I would regret it very much – you know, if it turned out that this was all forgotten, that somehow it was decided the Orphan should never be told, that one way or another it was more convenient to kick over the traces. Oh, then I would weep like a child in a storm. Then you would hear me screaming.

Cheng Ying How shall I tell Cheng Bo? The words will choke me.

Ghost of Gongsun Tell him the way you used to tell him stories. Paint a scroll for him to find.

Cheng Ying Where would I begin?

Ghost of Gongsun In a great city, not long ago, a weak and foolish young Emperor fell victim to a wily minister –

Cheng Ying – who built him a pleasure garden –

Ghost vanishes while Cheng Ying paints on.

– where he could indulge his every taste. When the Emperor began killing the people for his sport, the wiser ministers at the Court protested, but were defeated by that evil minister, who had become favourite.

I wonder how much Cheng Bo knows of this. A few weeks ago I would have said he knew nothing at all. But then I sent him on an important and difficult journey. There was no one else I could trust so well, and, besides, I wanted him to see something of the world beyond the Palace. He returned proud, justly proud, of his achievement, but with a reserve that I had never encountered in him before. When he showed me the plants he had found and talked about what he had observed in the mountains, he was still the enthusiastic child. But about the other things he had seen along the road he would not speak. For the first time, I found in him a reserve, a secrecy – a hint, even, of anger. And I wondered why he could not tell me what he had seen.

Cheng Bo Father, I shot two geese with a single arrow. Tu'an Gu says it is an omen.

Cheng Ying Surely it must be. I have never heard of such a thing.

Cheng Bo They fell in the garden of the Forbidden Palace, but Tu'an Gu said I might go in and fetch them.

Cheng Ying Nobody goes there.

Cheng Bo There was a guard. I could smell the wine on his breath. And he spoke of a Princess. What is this story you are painting?

Cheng Ying He spoke of a Princess. Did you believe him?

Cheng Bo As soon he mentioned her he became afraid, and begged me not to tell Tu'an Gu. Here is an Emperor, but he seems to be shooting arrows into a crowd. Why would that be?

Cheng Ying Did you believe the guard when he spoke of a Princess?

Cheng Bo Here is a ferocious dog attacking a courtier, but someone intervenes and kills the dog. And then –

Cheng Ying Of course if you had seen a Princess, that would be something. That would be proof.

Cheng Bo I saw a distraught old lady with matted hair, like the madwomen who dress up in old scraps of silk and ribbons and go shouting through the streets. But she spoke in the manner of the Court. Who was she? And who is this ferocious minister taking his sword to a baby?

Cheng Ying Ah! Do not ask me. Do not ask me about the child. And they told me the Princess had taken her own life for grief. Yet you saw the Princess in the Forbidden Palace, and Tu'an Gu was with you?

Cheng Bo He stayed outside. He said it seemed to be my destiny to enter.

Cheng Ying He should be afraid of your destiny.

Cheng Bo I myself am afraid of my destiny. I cannot see it. I do not know who I am. It is as if a thumb moves subtly across a scroll, and I glimpse the next moment in my life in the split second before that moment unfolds. The thumb moves. The great landscape is unfurled – the crags, the precipices, the winding road among the rocks, and then all these episodes of relentless cruelty: a man dashes his brains against a tree, a woman is beheaded, a child dismembered. You weep as you paint. You weep at what you ask me to see.

Cheng Ying My hand flies over the page. My tongue is the prisoner of my grief.

Cheng Bo I fear that I am not your son. Maybe I am the son of Tu'an Gu. Heaven help me if that is true. He is a detested man.

Cheng Ying You are not the son of Tu'an Gu. But it is true – you are not my son.

Cheng Bo Who am I, if I am not your son? I see you are telling a story for me. But will the story tell me who I am? Surely I have the right to know who I am?

Cheng Ying Look at your life in the scroll. Many have died for you. You are the massacre child. You are the Orphan of Zhao.

SCENE TWENTY-TWO
THE CAPTAIN OF THE GUARD

Wei Jiang approaches the Captain from behind, and grabs him suddenly around the neck.

Wei Jiang Captain of the Guard, whom do you serve?

Captain I serve the Emperor and his Chief Minister, the noble Tu'an Gu.

Wei Jiang Whose seal is this?

Captain I dare not say. I am a humble man, and I cannot read all the seal characters.

Wei Jiang You live at Court and you cannot recognise the characters of the Emperor himself?

Captain I am afraid. I do not know who you are, or why you come up on me in the night.

Wei Jiang I am Wei Jiang.

The Captain immediately prostrates himself.

Captain My General. There was a rumour you had come back to the city.

Wei Jiang The Emperor entrusted me with his seal of office. Whom do you serve?

Captain I am a loyal soldier. I serve the Emperor.

Wei Jiang The Emperor is dead. Whom will you serve now?

Captain My lord, order me and I shall obey.

Wei Jiang Go tell your men. Make the Palace secure.

SCENE TWENTY-THREE
THE PRINCESS AND THE ORPHAN

Just before dawn, the Orphan goes to the deserted Palace.
He carries a lantern.

Cheng Bo (*whispering*) Guard! Guard! Where is the guard? I am the man who came here yesterday. Do not be afraid. I must speak with the Princess. Guard!

Princess You will not rouse him like that. He is drunk as usual.

Cheng Bo Forgive me for waking you before dawn.

Princess You cannot wake me. I seldom sleep. Nothing seems to sleep here – the monkeys, the birds, the insects – everything chatters away through the night. Only the guard lies senseless with the liquor I distil for him from the wild paddy. But . . . you told me you would leave me in peace, and here you come again before dawn to torment me.

Cheng Bo I have a message. Your father the Emperor is dead. I am sorry to be the bearer of such news.

Princess If the Emperor is dead, that means I myself am not long for this world. The man you call your father will very soon have me done away with. I shall be strangled, I expect. When did the Emperor die?

Cheng Bo An hour ago.

Princess I wonder why it should have occurred to you to come here in the dark to tell me.

Cheng Bo Because I do not know if I shall survive today's events, and if I do not survive I shall at least have had the satisfaction of telling you something.

Princess That my father is dead? It is a grim satisfaction.

Cheng Bo I wanted to tell you that I believe you are my mother.

Princess I am a madwoman wandering at night through a palace full of monkeys. I cannot be your mother.

Cheng Bo I am the Orphan of Zhao. My dying father named me the Orphan of Zhao. Tell me I am the Orphan of Zhao! I may have to die today. I may have to kill today. But if I have to die, if I have to kill, at least I should know who I am, and how it comes that I was born for this bloodthirsty destiny. I am a young man whose body has not yet known love, but I must kill first. I must discharge this cruel obligation.

Princess Tell me whom you are obliged to kill. Tell me in plain words.

Cheng Bo I must kill Tu'an Gu, the father who adopted me.

Princess And why must you kill Tu'an Gu? Tell me simply, so that I can decide whether I am mad.

Cheng Bo Tu'an Gu killed my father, Zhao Dun, and all his clan.

Princess Forgive me but you have been somewhat misinformed. Tu'an Gu did not kill Zhao Dun. Speaking through a messenger, on my father the Emperor's behalf, Tu'an Gu gave him the choice of poison, dagger or the bowstring. Zhao Dun killed himself fearlessly, as he was obliged to do. He chose the dagger.

Cheng Bo Am I the Orphan of Zhao?

Princess The first time I saw you I knew at once you were the Orphan of Zhao. Only I feared that I had lost my reason.

Cheng Bo Then you are indeed my mother and I kneel to you.

Princess You are my son. I do not know how this has come about. I gave you to the doctor but they told me he betrayed you. Go now. I shall welcome you again when you have fulfilled your obligation.

SCENE TWENTY-FOUR
THE REVENGE

Gongs and bells are sounding throughout the Palace. There is a mass panic among the eunuchs. People are running in the direction of the audience room. Then they seem to hear something which sends them off in the opposite direction. There is confusion of another kind among the Palace Guard. They huddle together and pass on messages. It is dawning on them that there has been a coup: on the death of the Emperor, Wei Jiang has taken over the reins of government. He already has the loyalty and co-operation of the Palace Guard. The rest is a matter of time.

Tu'an Gu Officer, send me the Captain of the Guard. I said: Officer! Send me the Captain of the Guard. At once. Here. To the audience room.

The Officer, after a moment of hesitation, runs away, fast, without speaking.

He looked as if he had seen a ghost. Everyone is in shock. The Emperor must have died in the night, and I am the last to be informed. How could that have happened? Cheng Ying was supposed to give me a clear warning. We may have lost valuable time.

A group of Guards runs through the room. They ignore Tu'an Gu.

Captain of the Guard! I said: Captain! Send me the Captain of the Guard at once on pain of death. Do you not know who I am? I am Tu'an Gu!

Suddenly and without a word, a man runs up to him, slaps him in the face, hard, and runs off. The soldiers who have seen this do nothing about it. They also disperse fast. Then one of them runs back and slaps him again, as if as an afterthought.

They are telling me I am finished, just because the Emperor is dead. But I am not finished. I am Chief Minister. I still command the Palace Guard. Captain! Captain! Where is that drunken fool? Ah! Cheng Bo!

From one end of the empty audience room, the Orphan of Zhao contemplates Tu'an Gu, seeing him as if for the first time.

Cheng Ying is going to have some explaining to do. He promised me he would warn me if the Emperor's health went into a sudden decline. Now we have exactly the kind of hiatus I was intending to avoid. What a fool that old doctor is. But I'm glad you are here, and this is what I want you to do. Find the Captain of the Guard and tell him to report to me here. Then, as fast as possible, get as many of the ministers of state as you can track down, and tell them a council meeting will be held here in the audience room right away. So now be off with you. Quick.

The Orphan does nothing.

Are you dreaming? Is something wrong? We must act fast – everything depends on it. The Emperor's will was that I should succeed him to the throne. Perhaps you didn't know that. Perhaps I thought you were still too young to be told the secret. But you must have guessed that if I became Emperor, you, as my heir, as my son, my inheritor in all things, you too would . . . Did you think I was cutting you out? Why should I suddenly do that? You are my son. All the wealth I have amassed, all the power I have acquired, has been for you. Yet you look at me as if I were something detestable. Speak to me at least.

Cheng Bo Poison, the dagger, the bowstring – you gave my father a choice, and I bring the same choice for you. The common man would be glad to die by the ordinary hempen rope, if it should come to that – the end might be mercifully swift. The bowstring is stronger and sharper on the neck, and there is a fine bronze loop for the noose. It would be a quick death. The worst of the bowstring must be the anticipation. As for the poison, I found the plant myself, and was proud to identify it. But I never imagined putting it to such a test. No poison can be relied on to work in an instant. You may face a week of agony for which no remedy exists. Perhaps that is why my father chose the dagger. Courage is all a man needs, to take that remedy. And I am told my father had courage.

Tu'an Gu My son, my son, I do not understand this. What has happened? Has Cheng Ying killed himself?

Cheng Bo I am not your son. I am not the son of Cheng Ying. My father died long ago, before I was born. He killed himself at your command. He was the noble minister Zhao Dun. I am the Orphan of Zhao.

Tu'an Gu Two geese were killed with one arrow. Now the Emperor is dead and you bring me the bowstring and instruct me how to kill myself – the bowstring I myself ordered to be made for you. Here is the inscription on the bronze loop, with your name and mine together. Here is the gratitude of a son.

Cheng Bo You destroyed my father. You exterminated my clan. You did not rest until you were reassured you had killed me. Here then is the gratitude I owe you. I have brought you the three imperial punishments, three ways of escape from the the anger of the crowd. Choose now before the doors are battered down. For, make no mistake, no one here will be able to defend you from the mob, now that the Emperor is dead.

Tu'an Gu The people may hate me – they always hate a strong ruler. But they love you. It is in your power to protect me.

Cheng Bo I loved you once, and felt all the gratitude of a son. Be assured, I would have laid down my life to protect you. But for now my protection extends thus far and no further: I have persuaded the guard to let you die here by your own hand and in the manner of your choosing. If you delay, they will take you out and cast you alive on the mercy of the crowd.

Tu'an Gu You have conspired against me.

Noise.

What is that?

Cheng Bo It is the crowd. They have broken into the courtyard. Yes, there was a conspiracy. Only now am I learning the part I have played in it from the moment of my birth. The part I have still to play – that part is revealed to me with every step I take. I recognise myself in the eyes of others, in words and thoughts never contemplated by me. I had become a mystery to myself. Now by my actions I am solving the mystery.

Tu'an Gu Cheng Ying has lied to you. He has told you some story and, like a child, you have taken him at his word.

Cheng Bo Cheng Ying could have lied to me. China did not lie to me. I made a journey and I saw what I saw. I set out as a child. I crossed seven rivers twice over. Cruelty killed the child in me and left me with this mystery to solve.

Tu'an Gu Is it not most cruel to kill one who has been a father to you?

Cheng Bo I will not kill you unless you beg me to. The crowd will demand an answer from you, and they will make you pay at length for their suffering.

Noise.

Death is not always swift, as I learnt on my journey. Men squeal like pigs, and the worst of it is to see their shame – the secret and beautiful organs of the body tossed into the crowd. Men made eunuchs by eunuchs. Butchers butchering men, hands reaching into hot entrails, a peasant choked on his own liver, the child cut laughingly from the womb. None of this is strange to you, I think.

Tu'an Gu A ruler has to be cruel to be strong.

Cheng Bo Be strong now, be cruel and rule yourself. The gates have been forced, and the crowd is in the outer chamber. In a moment the guard will come and take you and throw you to your destiny. They are outnumbered and they have no choice in this matter. Here is the hunting knife you gave me. It is sharp.

Tu'an Gu Kill me. I am afraid. I dare not kill myself. Kill me quickly if ever you loved me.

Cheng Bo kills Tu'an Gu.

Cheng Bo I loved you once. Your fear has killed you. No one will fear you now.

The Palace Guard enter with Wei Jiang to carry off the body of Tu'an Gu. The Princess enters.

Wei Jiang Take that man's head and display it at the city gate.

Orphan of Zhao, turn now and greet the Princess, your mother.

Cheng Bo I cannot turn to her. I am ashamed to come before her in these bloodstained garments.

Princess Do not be ashamed. Each time I gaze on you, it is your father's face looks back at me. And that reminds me of his dying charge, to hide you well and keep you safe. To hide you well! How does a mother hide a weeping child – a lusty little pair of lungs? Each time I thought that I had failed to save you, I could so easily have killed myself. The pain, the fear would have been nothing to that grief. But then I would dream, and in my dream a child would be rattling the door, saying: 'Hide me, hide me, keep me safe!' So often I would rise from my bed and go to the door, and look out on the empty night. And as long as that hope kept rattling at the door, I could not kill myself. I could not fail you again, and say: 'My son, my son, I would keep you safe, but alas I have just killed myself.' I was obliged to live. I could no longer bear to sleep.

Cheng Bo And when I visited you, you were awake and waiting. Oh hide me now, my royal mother, hide me now, and keep me from the terror of my own revenge.

The Orphan turns to the Princess, who enfolds him in her sleeves.

SCENE TWENTY-FIVE
THE SONG OF THE DEAD

Ballad-Singer (*sings*)
  Ah
  Mother, the dead,
  Mother, the dead are deafening now.

The dead are like starlings in a tree.
    I clap my hands once.
    They rise in the air.
    They rise in a flock.
    They darken the sky.
    They turn on the wing.
    They turn again on the wing.
Mother, the dead are calling to me

Singing

Ah
Mother, the dead,
Mother, the dead are deafening now.
The dead have come back to the tree.
    I clap my hands again.
    They talk among themselves.
    I raise my bow to the sky.
    They turn their backs to my bow.
    I shoot arrows at the dead.
    All my arrows fall short.
Mother, the dead are laughing at me

Singing

Ah
Mother, the dead,
Mother, the dead are deafening now.
The dead are like starlings in a tree.
    They call me by my name.
        They call me by another name.
        They tell me my mother is dead.
        They tell me she is angry with me.
        They tell me who to love.
        They tell me who to kill.
Mother, the dead are deafening me

Singing

Ah
Mother, the dead,
Mother, the dead are deafening me.
    They tell me who to love.
    They tell me who to kill.
Mother, the dead are deafening me.

SCENE TWENTY-SIX
THE GHOST AND THE GRAVE

Cheng Ying This is the tree. And here are the steps cut in the rock. Nobody comes here any more – I can see that. Now where are the tombs? It should be here to the right – my child's grave.

Ghost All the tombs of your family were dug up long ago. Did nobody tell you? They were all desecrated.

Cheng Ying But my son's grave. It was a small thing.

Ghost They were thorough.

Cheng Ying They hated my son? He was a baby.

Ghost They hated you. You hated your son.

Cheng Ying No father hates his own baby son. Why should I be different?

Ghost That's what I have asked myself these eighteen years.

Cheng thinks about this for a moment.

Cheng Ying You knew my son? You seem too young to have known him.

Ghost I am your son. You betrayed me. You had me killed. You loved the Orphan of Zhao. You hid him and you cherished him. You brought him up as your own, and under the protection of the Court. It always makes me weep to think about it.

The Ghost weeps copiously.

Why did you hate me? Why did you love the Orphan of Zhao?

Cheng Ying Here is the tree. Here are the steps cut in the rock. Maybe the graves are a little further on. I am an old man now, and perhaps I have begun to forget. But I cannot remember ever having hated my son. If I had hated my son, it seems to me I should have remembered that. I should have asked myself what had made me such a monster of nature as to hate my son.

Ghost You loved the Orphan of Zhao. You gave him everything. I came to the courtyard at night and I watched him at play. I saw how he grew in your love. You gave him toys. You painted stories for him. Everybody loved him – and rightly so, he was a beautiful child. But can you not see how hurtful that was to me? You forgot me for the Orphan of Zhao. You forgot me out here on the hillside – a handful of scattered bones, white in the frost.

Cheng Ying Here is the tree. I am starting again from the tree. And here are the steps cut in the rock. But now I am an old man and I shall need your help. Show me the grave. You must help me die at your grave.

Ghost You do not deserve to find my grave.

Cheng Ying It is true – I deserve nothing. I am asking for what I do not deserve. I can see that I wronged you long ago, and the truth is: I cannot remember why. I feel there must have been a reason. I feel that I could have had no choice. But I cannot any longer tell you what the reason was. I am an old man and I am asking you to help me.

Ghost You are standing on my grave. Those three short scratches in the rock are where the workmen aimed thei picks when they destroyed my little home. There is nothing else to see.

Cheng Ying My wronged son, my love, place your cold hand here in the fold of my gown, and show me how to hold the knife. I do not lack courage but I doubt my strength and skill. Help me to die.

Ghost The moon is sharp on the blade. Hold it here below the rib. And if you do truly love me, I shall taste it in your heart's blood.

Cheng Ying Place your hand on my hand. Help me direct the blade.

Ghost There.

The Ghost tastes the heart's blood.

You love me. You always *did* love me.

And now you belong to me for ever.

Ends.